Wood Turning

BARRON'S

Original title of the book in Spanish: *Torno*
© Parramón Ediciones, S.A., 1999. World Rights
Published by Parramón Ediciones, S.A., Barcelona, Spain

Text: Vicenç Gibert and Josep López
Step-by-step: Rafael Martinez
Series design: Carlos Bonet
Photography: Nos & Soto

Translated from the Spanish by Michael Brunelle
and Beatriz Cortabarria

All inquiries should be addressed to:
Barron's Educational Series, Inc.
250 Wireless Blvd.
Hauppauge, NY 11788
http://www.barronseduc.com

Library of Congress Catalog Card No.: 00-101641
International Standard Book No. 0-7641-5245-9

Printed in Spain

987654321

CONTENTS

Introduction   5

Starting out

The turner's trade   6

Wood and related materials   8

Commonly used tools   10

Techniques

Preliminary steps   12

Spindle turning   14

Open-ended turning   18

Turning half pieces   22

Finishing on the lathe   26

Projects

Mirror frame   28

Cigar container   32

Small table   38

Wooden ball   44

Garden urn   50

Stool   56

Glossary   64

INTRODUCTION

The craft of the woodturner is one of creating a specific shape from a piece of wood that is turning on a lathe. Watching a turner while he or she works is like being at a magic show, because he or she changes a formless piece of wood into an absolutely perfect, beautiful and harmonious object.

The turner's job, like the jobs of all artisans, requires experience, ability, and patience. It is one of the most ancient trades known; it has always been linked to the trade of the cabinetmaker, since both participate in the task of creating furniture. The turner is usually involved in creating the stronger structural elements of furniture, like the legs of a chair or table, and in the decoration, creating applied decorative elements like half pieces. Nevertheless, they are capable of making complete pieces of furniture like tables, some chairs and garden urns, and pieces like bowls, lamp bases, and kitchen utensils.

Despite this, during the last few decades artisan turners have been pushed into second place by machines that can be operated by a single person and that are able to work wood horizontally and vertically and manufacture identical pieces in a very short amount of time.

In this volume, we explain all aspects related to wood turning that could be of interest either to a person who is starting out in this wonderful trade or to one who already has a certain degree of experience. In the first part we introduce the best woods for turning, a traditional lathe, the most commonly used cutting tools for both spindle turning and for faceplate work, and the results of applying a finish to the piece like polishing, waxing, or burning. Then we explain step by step how to make complete pieces or parts that are used to make a piece of furniture, so that the reader can begin to learn how to work at the lathe and create models similar to those in the projects.

This book is intended to be an homage to all turners who, despite the difficulties of the industrialized world, continue working in the traditional way, using their magic touch on the wood and converting it into true works of art.

Vicenç Gibert i Armengol

THE TURNER'S TRADE

The process of shaping wood has its origins in wood carving. The lathe was developed from mechanizing the process or the use of some kind of tool that caused the piece of wood to move at a certain speed. The antiquity of the turner's trade can be proven by observing the furniture of the Renaissance, the Baroque, the Neoclassic Period, and Modernism, because turned parts appear in pieces of all these styles. The master turner is a person who is capable of developing, with the ability of his own hands and little else, wood pieces in geometric and cylindrical shapes, and often with varying curves, that in many cases deserve to be called works of art.

Wood turning is a trade that consists of shaping pieces of wood using the rotational movement of the lathe and the able intervention of the master turner. A lathe is needed to rotate the piece of wood that is being shaped. The basic tools used for turning are gouges and chisels.

The earliest known lathes were rotated by means of a pedal that the turner controlled with his foot.

The turning speed was slow, but this fact allowed the creation of such complex cylindrical pieces as spiral columns. This type of work cannot be done with modern lathes because of their high rotational speed, which makes it impossible for the turner to control the spiral forms.

The workshop

All wood turning shops should have enough space to accommodate the lathe's supporting bench. The benches are usually long and made of wood, with metal legs anchored to the floor, and with a front space that allows the turner's gouges and chisels to be laid out in order. There also has to be enough surrounding space and light to allow the work to take place. In the past, wood turning shops did not have a means of collecting dust and wood shavings. But today, few shops are without dust collectors, because the turning process generates such a great amount of sawdust and shavings. For this reason, you'll definitely need to invest in a broom and dust pan.

The lathe

A lathe, by definition, is a machine in which work is rotated about a horizontal axis and shaped by a fixed tool. It consists of the following five basic components —the headstock, the motor and pulleys, the tailstock and the tool rest.

Even now you can still find two kinds of lathes coexisting. On the one hand is the traditional kind, manually driven, constructed with each and every part needed to turn different shapes in wood, that is to say, the headstock where the piece is attached at one end, the tailstock that holds the other end, and the four-step pulley that causes it to turn. On the other hand, the more modern lathes are run by a motor, have all the basic parts of the artisan's lathe, and substantially improve the efficiency of the work and make the turner's job easier.

The headstock

One of the most important parts of the lathe is the headstock, which is located to the left side of the lathe. It permits the attachment of the parts that in turn hold the wood that is to be turned. These parts are the spur center, for turning long

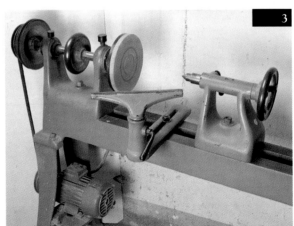

1. An artisanal wood turning shop. The overhead belts power the lathes in the shop.

2. The tools are placed on the bench in the front of the lathe, to help the turner work efficiently.

3. A modern lathe. You can see its metal structure and at the far left the variable speed belt driven by the motor.

pieces; the faceplate for large, flat or hollow pieces; and the three-jawed chuck or the universal chuck, which is used for hollowing and turning pieces that are not very large like doorknobs or box lids. Other useful attachments for holding wood in the lathe include the screw chuck, which will hold wood up to 4" thick, and the spigot chuck, specially designed for turning the end grain of cylinders, which is useful when making boxes with lids and vases or urn-shaped pieces.

The drive

The drive consists of a motor designed for long periods of work, enclosed in a metal shell to protect it from wood shavings and sawdust. The motor turns the headstock by means of a belt that is attached to a four-step pulley.

The speed at which the motor turns the lathe can vary from 1,000 to 5,000 revolutions per minute. The choice of speed basically depends on the size of the piece that is to be turned and the hardness of the wood, for example, a slow speed for large, hard pieces, and a faster speed for small, soft pieces.

Tailstock

The tailstock is a moveable element that together with the headstock allows a piece of wood to be attached between two points to be able to do spindle turning.

The tailstock consists of a strong metal structure that should be able to slide back and forth smoothly. The center should be removable by unscrewing it with your hand.

Tool rest

The tool rest lets you brace your tools against a sturdy surface. There should be levers that can clamp the tool rest at a desired height to facilitate the turning operation. There are bar supports for turning longer pieces and T-shaped supports that can be used for turning pieces of wood on the faceplate.

4. Notice, at the far right, the headstock with its threaded drive spindle, into which has been mounted a spur center.

5. The piece of wood is screwed to the faceplate so it can be turned.

6. The blank is attached to the lathe using the universal chuck to begin removing material.

7. Illustration of the motor and the different four-step pulleys and the belt that drive the headstock.

8. The tailstock of a traditional lathe. It should slide easily along the lathe bed. Notice the hand wheel, which allows the point to move.

9. The tool rest mounting bracket will accept tool rests of different lengths depending on the piece that is to be turned. This type of tool rest is used for turning long pieces.

10. The T-shaped support, with a quick release lever that allows the turning of small pieces.

WOOD AND RELATED MATERIALS

Wood is the most appropriate material for making turned objects. Turners favor elm and sycamore the most of all the species of wood. It is also important to point out that within a particular species there is a great variation among different pieces of the same wood.

If the wood that you wish to turn contains a lot of minerals, a shower of sparks will be produced when applying the tool. If the wood contains a lot of moisture, it may be easier to turn than dry wood, but you run the risk of cracking as the wood dries.

Another important aspect when selecting wood is to keep in mind that some kinds, when being turned, emit an unpleasant odor, and can even irritate the upper respiratory system.

For these reasons, the turner should test the wood he or she is going to turn. By using a piece of the same wood to be turned, different cuts can be made to see how workable it may be.

Some fine-grained hardwoods, like mahogany, sapele, and walnut, are chosen for their ease of working on the lathe, and because they are woods that take a beautiful finish and make elegant furniture.

Oak, ash, elm, and chestnut are also hardwoods, but they are more porous and therefore not as fine-grained.

Fir is a wood with very colorful, beautiful graining; it is very solid, not as heavy and more durable than oak. Nevertheless, the highest quality hardwood is, by far, ebony. It is a dense, hard, and heavy wood. There are several species; the most well known come from the Congo. Birch, beech, and all varieties of pine tend to be lighter and less durable. They are commonly used for making less expensive furniture.

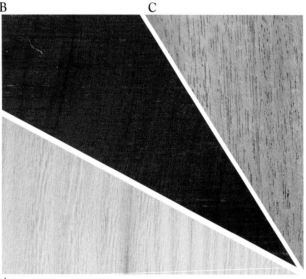

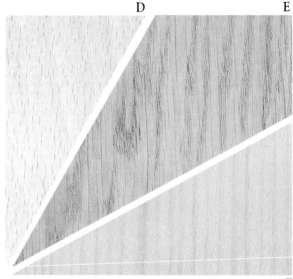

A. Cypress is a grainy wood of a yellowish color that belongs to the pine family. It has perennial leaves, always green, with fine straight fibers and reddish color. The cypress grows to a majestic size and has a conical form.

B. Ebony is one of the heaviest woods in existence and has an intense black color. It is especially used as a decorative wood whose outstanding characteristics are its solid structure, durability, and weight. Its fibers are fine and take polish well.

C. Mahogany has three characteristics that make it immediately recognizable: great weight, compactness, and dark red color. It can also have other colors according to the species. Mahogany mainly comes from South and Central America, specifically from Cuba, and has excellent workability. It has a very fine grain and is easy to polish, it accepts varnish and wax very well, and furthermore it does not warp nor is it susceptible to attack by wood-boring insects. It is used in manufacturing high-end furniture.

D. Recently cut beech is very white; after some time and when it is completely dry, it turns a reddish-gray color. This wood has three drawbacks: it twists, warps, and rots. It abounds in Spain, in the mountainous regions of the northwest; it is also found throughout Europe. It is easy to work whether manually or mechanically.

E. Oak is used in construction because it becomes harder when it is wet. Furthermore, its weight and durability make it a favorite of wood turners. Its coloring is mainly gray. It is found in Spain and North America. Oak is prone to attacks by wood-boring insects. Varieties include the holm oak and the cork oak.

F. Fir is a wood noted for its even grain and is therefore very easy to work. It is white in color, with long, straight fibers. There is a notable difference between the annual rings of the spring wood and the autumn wood. Fir is often confused with the wood of a pine tree, which is very similar; however, pine has more knots.

Wax and paraffin

Other basic materials that are used in wood turning are waxes and paraffin; these help create a finish on the wood that is handsome and pleasing to the touch. Pure beeswax can be used to apply a fine natural finish on wood. To apply it the lathe should be left turning and the wax or paraffin should be pressed against the wood causing it to melt. Then pressure is applied with a cheesecloth or a cotton cloth to achieve the desired gloss and beauty.

Additional elements

Besides looking at wood as the basic material of wood turning, or at the waxes used to achieve a good finish, it is worth examining some of the small turned pieces that, as auxiliary elements, allow us to complement furniture of all styles.

Knobs, rings, balusters, and decorative pieces are made on the lathe and are used as decorative details. Although they can be made of other materials, like metal and plastic, wood continues to be the most commonly used material for making these pieces.

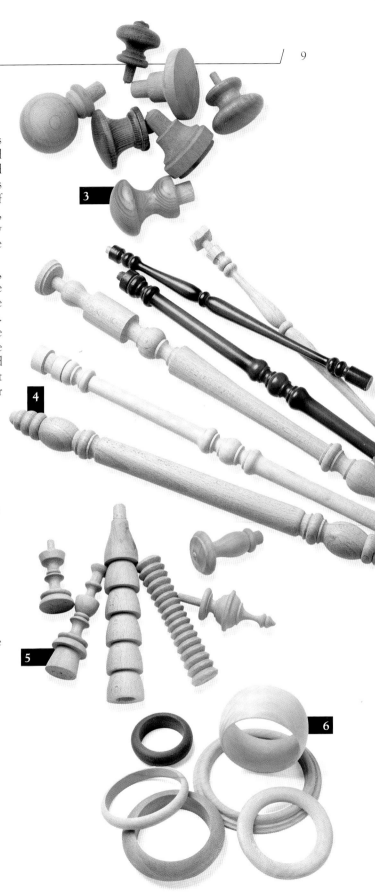

1. Wax and paraffin are the base of numerous finishes in wood turning. Cheesecloth or a cotton cloth allows you to achieve a fine finish.

2. It is important to have different grades of sandpaper to be able to sand and smooth the wood easily.

3. The types and styles of these knobs show off the wood they are made of. Often multiple pieces are made using motorized lathes or copying machines.

4. Balusters are other elements that are used as decorative pieces on furniture. There are several other shapes that can be adapted to different furniture.

5. Samples of turned pieces that are used as ornaments on furniture.

6. Different types of rings. Turners prefer to make several at a time. Preparing the material, sharpening the tools, and setting up the lathe for making a single ring is not practical.

COMMONLY USED TOOLS

Turning tools are the fundamental instruments of the turner. They are used for roughing out, shaping and hollowing the wood. But the turner should also have other useful tools to make the work easier.

Other than cutting tools, there are three main groups of tools needed for woodturning: those used for marking, measuring, and checking; tools for striking and pulling; and those for specialized tasks such as angled legs or making threads in the wood.

Tools for marking and measuring

It is very important to have a collection of instruments to use for marking, measuring, and checking the object that is being turned. The turner also needs tools to transfer dimensions from one part to another.

Among the most used instruments for measuring and marking are calipers for checking the thickness, lengths, or inside dimensions of a piece, as well as squares, marking gauges, awls and rulers. Sometimes a turner may devise his or her own tool for a specific purpose or project.

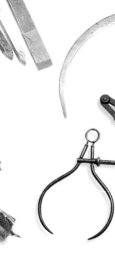

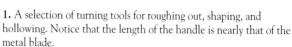

1. A selection of turning tools for roughing out, shaping, and hollowing. Notice that the length of the handle is nearly that of the metal blade.

2. In order, from top to bottom: roughing gouge with a medium flute, used for roughing out the wood; a spear point chisel, used for deep cuts in the wood; a skew chisel used for faceplate turning; and a chisel used for cutting the end grain or shaping.

3. Bits for drills and bits with handles made by the turner himself for boring holes in the face of wood pieces.

4. Calipers are fundamental for frequently checking the diameter of a part being turned. They are also used to measure length, thickness, and inside dimensions. It is advisable to have calipers of various sizes.

Tools for shaping wood

Turning tools is a generic term for various tools with approximately an 8-inch (20 cm) hard wood handle and a long metal blade sharpened at the end. They can be used for removal of stock as well as for shaping parts. Metal drill bits, which are used with a wood handle for boring holes in the wood, also belong to this group.

5. Another group of tools used for measuring and marking consists of a square and a marking gouge, which is used for marking wood, a ruler for taking measurements, a scratch awl for making holes in the wood, and a pencil with a medium hard lead.

6. The turner is skilled at making templates for reproducing designs. These consist of a piece of wood with a series of nails inserted in the edge spaced according to the design of the desired profile.

Gauges

These are used to check the sizes of wood cylinders with small diameters.

They are usually made of sheet metal, which has a series of cutouts of different dimensions.

Tools for striking and pulling

The hammer is basically used to attach or fix the wood to the lathe. The adjustable wrench, which is used for changing the headstock and tailstock centers, is also included in the group of striking or pulling tools.

Tools for specific tasks

In this group are tools used for specific tasks. A special clamp allows the turning of angled wood parts. This tool is made up of a piece of wood that attaches to the lathe and a screw vise for clamping the piece of wood that is to be turned. The tap and thread chaser are instruments used to cut male and female threads in wood.

7. Gauges are practical instruments used to check small diameters quickly.

8. Large hammers are used to strike large pieces of wood, while small ones are used for medium and small pieces of wood.

9. The adjustable wrench is needed to change the different centers on the lathe.

10. This clamp is an indispensable tool used for turning angled legs. Notice the shape of the wrench that is used for tightening.

11. There are two threading tools: the tap (below), which is used for making female threads, and the thread chaser (above), which is used for making male threads.

PRELIMINARY STEPS

Choosing the wood

One of the first steps in wood turning is choosing the wood, whose main characteristics should be beauty, strength, and ease of working.

The turner must be careful not to choose a species of wood that is too hard. Examples of such woods are elm or teak, which are known for wearing down the cutting edges of wood turning tools because of their hardness.

Also, the turner should make sure that the level of moisture in the wood is not high, so that it will be easier to work and to avoid the appearance of cracks in the wood.

Wood does not always come from lumberyards. Sometimes round posts or railroad ties are used. In such cases, it is necessary to check for nails and staples and to remove them so that the piece can be turned without damaging the tools.

Patterns

Generally, traditional turners do not need to make patterns. They have spent long hours learning woodturning craftsmanship through hands-on work as apprentices. However, it is recommended that beginning woodturners use sketches or shop drawings when making projects, as they are an aid in checking dimensions and transferring them to the turned piece. Once the pieces have been made, they can be compared to the shop drawing to check for accuracy.

Marking

After selecting an appropriate piece of wood, we go on to the task of preparing it for the turning process. If the chosen block of wood is to be turned between two points (or spindle turned), the centers of each end of the piece of wood must be located and marked. These marks indicate the points where the blank will be attached to the lathe. Using a pencil and a straight edge, the turner will proceed to draw diagonal lines connecting opposite corners on each end of the piece of wood. The points where the diagonals cross will indicate the centers. Next, holes should be made at the intersections with an awl, to make it easier to mount the piece of wood in the lathe.

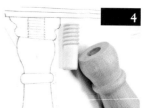

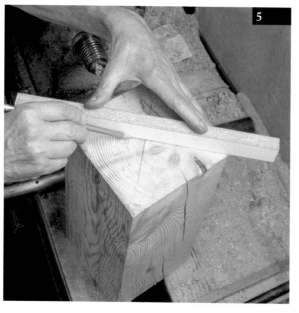

1. It is important to select the appropriate wood.

2. In some cases, as in cutting profiles or replacing or adding parts, patterns make the work easier.

3. It is easy to mark the piece using a shop pattern drawn to full scale on a board.

4. Once they have been turned, the pieces should be checked against the drawing for accuracy.

5. To find the center, diagonal lines are drawn from corner to corner on the block of wood.

6. A mark is made with an awl at the point where the diagonal lines cross.

Placing the piece in the lathe

After the centers of the piece have been marked, it is placed in the lathe between the headstock and the tailstock. The headstock holds the piece of wood so that it can be turned.

When using large pieces or hard woods, several taps with the hammer on the wood will help set the spur center and will guarantee that it stays attached to the machine. You should be aware that a piece of wood can come off the lathe when it is turning. If you are careful in mounting the piece to the lathe, there should be no problems.

Next, the tailstock is slid along the bed of the lathe and the point pushed into the mark on the other end of the piece. Once this has been done, the tailstock is tightened to the bed to keep it from moving, and then the live point is adjusted to the piece of wood using the hand wheel, until the blades of the spur center are forced into the wood. Sometimes the wheel at the tailstock can be backed out one half turn to lessen the pressure, and then locked into position using the quick release lever.

8

7. The turner uses a hammer to tap the wood block to attach it to the headstock. He uses the previously marked lines to center the piece.

7

Attaching the tool rest

When the piece of wood has been locked into the lathe, either the long bar or T-bar tool rest is attached, depending on the type of project that is being done.

The height at which the tool rest should be set depends on the edge of the gouge, but as long as the turner feels comfortable and the tool is sharp, the exact height is not very important. Take note of the space between the tool rest and the piece of wood. The space between them should be between 1/8 inch and 3/16 inch (3 or 4 mm) for better control of the tool and to reduce the risk of catching the fingers between the tool rest and the wood. Before turning on the lathe, turn the piece around by hand to make sure that the wood will not hit the tool rest.

9

8. Attaching the tailstock to the end of the piece of wood.

9. A tool rest that allows working with relatively long pieces of wood is attached. Resting the gouges here will help them to properly work the wood.

SPINDLE TURNING

The term spindle turning describes the technique of attaching a piece of wood at each end, between the live center and the headstock. This technique is recommended for beginning woodturners until they acquire skill and confidence. More complex methods will be covered later.

When using the spindle turning method all kinds of turning tools can be used, but keep in mind that a much finer finish will be achieved by using tools with cutting edges rather than scrapers.

In this section two clearly different phases are covered: one is the roughing out of the wood, which fundamentally consists of removing material and turning a piece with a square cross section into a cylinder; the other is shaping, which is based on making the necessary cuts to achieve the desired silhouette.

Our first project on page 28 demonstrates the spindle turning technique in which the roughing out and shaping operations are demonstrated. A second exercise shows the making of an angled leg, in which we use a special technique for mounting the piece in the lathe.

Shaped base

To demonstrate what is involved in the spindle turning technique let's use a shaped base as an example. Once the piece is correctly and securely mounted in the lathe, the first step of the task consists of converting the square cross section of the wood into a cylinder, in other words, roughing out the piece.

Roughing out

To accomplish the roughing out, a task that is always the first step in turning wood, a roughing gouge is used. The gouge should be braced on the tool rest, and the blade supported with the left hand. This way, the gouge can be moved forward keeping the concave side facing in the direction that it is moving. The right hand holds the handle of the tool to counterbalance the leverage caused by the motion of the piece of wood. If the lathe is stopped, a series of ripples will be seen. Remember that for now you are only interested in making a rough cylinder. The tool should always be held slightly sideways and pointed in the direction of its movement.

The cut is initiated by gently pushing the tool forward, while trying to keep the cutting edge tangent to the circumference of the cut.

The movement of the tool should go from left to right or vice versa. If the surface becomes wavy while spindle turning with the roughing gouge, it can be corrected by watching the top edge of the piece. Keep in mind that if a chisel is used, the finish will be smoother as long as it is used without scraping the wood.

1. Notice how the turner holds the roughing gouge when roughing out the piece.

2. When the lathe is stopped, you can see how the piece is taking on the shape of a rough cylinder, with rounded edges.

3. Continue roughing out the piece, holding the roughing gouge slightly sideways and angled, until a cylinder is created.

4. Notice the rippled surface of the turned piece.

Shaping

Once the piece has been made into a rough cylinder, you can begin to shape it and to remove material with the same roughing gouge.

It is important to move the tool towards the area where the material is to be removed, tightly holding the cutting end and angling it slightly sideways towards the direction in which it is moving.

Successive passes should be made from left to right; angling the tool in the same manner as just described. Again, when the tool is moved from right to left, it must be held very tightly.

Once the rough shaping of the block of wood has been done, a parting tool or scraper can be used to round the ends of the piece, using the same spindle turning technique. The tool is manipulated in the same way, but in this case, only a small movement of the left wrist is made to move the chisel.

5. The shaping can also be done using the roughing gouge.

6. Moving the tool in the direction of the cut.

7. Notice how the thumb helps to firmly hold the tool in position to guarantee safety while removing material.

8. Notice how the position of the gouge has changed, at the same time the thumb is rested on the concavity of the tool.

9. Turning the ends of the wood with a chisel or scraper.

Angled chair leg

In all trades, there are techniques that have an added level of complexity, that without a doubt allow the creation of very beautiful pieces. In this case, continuing with the spindle turning technique, the making of an angled chair leg is demonstrated.

To make this a special clamp is needed, which allows the woodturner to mount the piece of wood while maintaining the linearity between the two attachment points of the lathe. The clamp is attached to the piece that will be turned, and a special wrench is used to tighten it. Note that the manner of turning the wood and the tools that are used are the same as in the shaped base project, but there is an added level of difficulty.

The woodturner begins the task by attaching the piece of wood using the special clamp. As we mentioned in the section on preliminary tasks, in order to attach the piece to the lathe it must be tapped lightly with a hammer so you can be assured that the piece is centered on the lathe. The clamp is especially useful because it allows you to maintain the linearity between the attachment points on the piece. The risk in doing this kind of turning comes in the rotation, which has spinning angles all along the piece. The turner must be careful to avoid being struck by one of the angles.

Roughing out

The turning can be started using a chisel or a gouge and, with the aid of a previously prepared template, the areas of the piece that are being turned can be marked. Here the wood is roughed out using the roughing gouge, turning the square piece of wood into a cylinder.

The method of holding the tools and their positioning are done in the same way as they are in spindle turning.

10. Notice the leg, belonging to a chair, that has an angled rather than a straight line.

11. Attaching the piece of wood to the lathe using a hammer.

12. The piece is mounted in the lathe. Notice the angle formed by the wood that is to be turned.

13. The length that is to be turned is marked. The piece will have a straight section that will allow the joining of the leg to the seat rail.

Shaping

A scraping tool is used to shape the profiles in the same way as explained in the section on shaping the base profile, and scraping is carefully begun using the sharp point.

Shaping of the middle area of the leg is finished using the medium gouge. This tool will create a much smoother finish than the parting tool or the scraper.

Once half of the leg is completed, the piece is turned around and again mounted on the lathe, attaching the clamp to the previously turned part. The piece is mounted in the same way as previously described.

Sometimes, when the pieces are too long, an auxiliary support is used that keeps the wood from vibrating as it turns. However, the wood turning process can continue without any interruption, since the side near the tool rest is not obstructed. Angled turned pieces can be produced by following this procedure, thanks to the special clamp that allows the mounting of the piece to the lathe, without causing any displacement between the two points of support.

14. Removing material with the medium gouge.

15. The piece is shaped with the parting tool. In this case, it is necessary to twist the wrist slightly while holding the tool firmly.

16. Then the shaping is completed using the medium gouge.

17. Once half the leg is finished, the piece is turned around in the lathe.

18. The auxiliary support that keeps the piece from vibrating.

19. Notice how the finished piece looks.

OPEN-ENDED TURNING

Open-ended turning is done by attaching the piece of wood that is to be turned at one of its ends. Usually, when you wish to use this technique, you should pay attention to the direction of the grain of the wood.

It takes much skill to use a roughing gouge for open-ended turning. It is much simpler for the beginner to use a parting tool or scraper. The most important thing to remember about these tools is that they should always be pointing downward.

Hollowing

First we demonstrate a hollowing project to show the detailed steps and techniques used. Just as its name indicates, hollowing consists of removing material from a piece of wood much like a bowl.

To begin hollow turning it is necessary to prepare a cylindrical piece of wood with one end reduced to fit into the cup chuck of the lathe. When the diameter of the spigot is determined to be correct by checking with calipers, the cylinder can be inserted into the cup chuck.

Lathes often have accessories that can be used to mount pieces of wood of various shapes and sizes. Screw chucks are one of the simplest, consisting of a threaded screw that is inserted into a hole drilled onto the end of the blank that is to be turned. This type of chuck will only work with short pieces of wood. The three-jaw chuck has long been popular with wood turners. The jaws will grip a spigot or cylindrical shape from the outside, and can also expand to grip a hollow piece of wood from the inside. The cup chuck is ideally suited to the type of piece used in this example.

When the piece has been mounted in the cup chuck, it is tapped several times with a hammer to make sure that it is attached well. At this point it is advisable to turn the lathe by hand to verify that the piece is centered. It is important that the piece be firmly mounted, because an unstable piece of wood will cause difficulties during the turning process. The tool rest should be placed in front of the face that is to be worked.

The hollowing of the wood is done using the roughing gouge, which creates large wood shavings and quickly removes a great amount of wood. The hollowing can be done from the center working to the outside, or starting at the edge and cutting towards the center. The intent is to make the inside walls perpendicular to the base of the turned piece, so the spear point chisel is used to widen the inside of the piece. Keep in mind that as the walls are made thinner, they also become weaker.

To check the depth of the piece, place a simple piece of straight wood across the rim and measure the distance to the bottom of the hollowed piece using a ruler.

A spear point chisel is used to remove the wood from the lathe, cutting into the piece until it is attached only by a small amount of material at the center.

When it is determined that the piece is completely hollowed, you can finish removing material from the bottom. A square end chisel can be used to do this. In this case it was necessary to move the tool rest to work on the side of the piece.

Before completely removing the wood, the decorative beads should be made using the chisel.

1. The diameter of the spigot must fit into the cup chuck.

2. The cylinder is removed and the cup chuck put in place.

3. The wood is mounted in the cup chuck.

4. The wood is hollowed out with the roughing gouge.

5. The inside walls are made perpendicular to the base using the spear point chisel.

6. Front view shows the thickness of the walls and that they are perpendicular to the base.

7. Checking the depth of the cut.

8. The spear point chisel is used to remove wood to be able to separate the piece from the lathe.

9. The bottom of the piece is finished using a square end chisel.

10. Finally, the decorative beads are made using the chisel.

Hollow turning

One type of open-ended turning technique consists of turning a part without actually hollowing it. To better understand this technique we demonstrate how to turn a lid with a knob in the center. The wood we used is a light colored cypress with pronounced graining.

The exercise begins with the blank already mounted in the lathe. One of the basic tools used in this technique is the roughing gouge. It can be used to make very fine cuts, especially when the part is being chuck turned. Notice that the wood shavings it makes here are very small.

As the tool moves towards the center, it changes directions to begin shaping the knob. The correct angle of the tool is necessary to control the cutting of the wood. If the gouge is angled down it will not only scratch the wood, but will not produce a fine cut.

The square chisel is used when detailed cuts are required in hard to reach areas.

It is important to use the right chisels for the desired effects. Keep in mind that tools of different sizes are used to create profiles of different dimensions. A square chisel is used for turning in narrow areas, where the wood can be removed using the sharp corner.

Although we are focused on the techniques of hollow turning, we must not forget to check the diameter of the part. The outside calipers are used for this.

To remove the piece from the lathe, the wood is first removed with the parting tools and then we continue to cut away material with the square chisel. When the time comes to cut the piece off, the lathe can be turned off as pressure is applied with the cutting edge of the tool. This way the wood will come off without posing any danger.

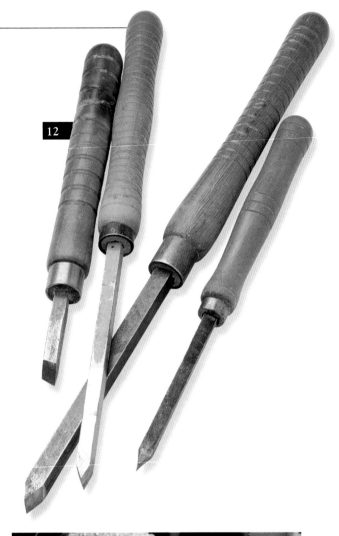

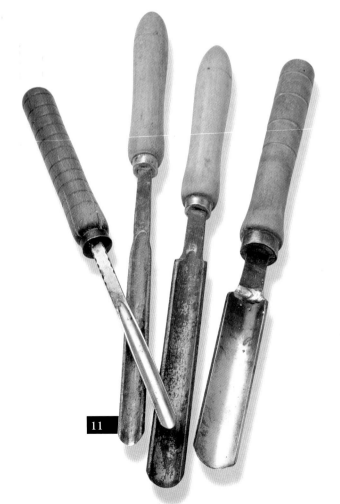

11. The roughing out is done with the fluted gouge.

12. The square chisel is used for making fine cuts.

13. The fluted gouge is held firmly and braced on the tool rest while sliding across it in a perpendicular direction.

14. Notice the angle of the tool as it meets the wood.

15. See how the tool is held; the index finger is under the tool rest applying pressure.

16. It is easy to cut tight areas with a square chisel.

17. The fluted gouge is used to turn the outside of the knob.

18. Checking the diameter of the part.

19. The part is cut off the lathe with the square chisel.

TURNING HALF PIECES

Another unique use of the lathe is to turn a piece of wood and then divide it in half so it can be used as a decorative appliqué on furniture.

The first step is designing the profile of the part that will be turned. The drawing should be made on a piece of wood, which will later be used for transferring the dimensions to the part on the lathe. In order to make halves, a cabinetmaker must prepare the wood pieces and apply glue to both, placing a sheet of newsprint in between them that will later allow them to be separated. The pieces are held together with clamps until the glue is dry to guarantee good adhesion.

Turning half pieces is done using the spindle turning technique; therefore, the wood piece to be turned will be attached at both ends. Material is removed using the roughing gouge. This tool should be used whenever you are beginning to turn a rectangular piece, because any type of flat chisel will create splinters and may weaken the wood. Once a cylinder is created, the shaping of the profile can be done with a square chisel. This tool is used because it easily makes fine, precise cuts.

Whatever the wood being turned or the technique being used, it is always easier if the design of the turned piece is at hand. The turner usually places it in front so it can be easily seen. The fluted gouge is used to shape the wood and whenever it is appropriate for the profile; in this case we use a medium size gouge. Remember that the finish created by this tool is much finer and smoother than that of the skew chisel. When doing spindle turning, the length of the piece being turned will determine the kind of tool rest that will be used.

Sandpaper is used to achieve a good, smooth finish. The turner applies more or less pressure on the piece to create an even surface. In this case a wax finish is applied to the wood.

While the lathe is turning, a piece of beeswax or paraffin is applied directly to the wood, so the friction melts the wax and causes it to penetrate the wood. The gloss is brought out by buffing the piece with a cotton cloth.

The finished piece is separated very carefully. The cutting edge of a square chisel is worked into the seam between the two pieces of wood. When the blade has been inserted into the wood, both are lifted and struck against the work bench. Here can be seen the importance of the role of the newsprint, which keeps the two parts from completely adhering to each other.

Even though they are glued together, the paper makes it easy to separate them. When the tool goes farther into the wood, the two separate completely. The newsprint stays glued to the two halves of wood.

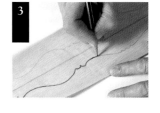

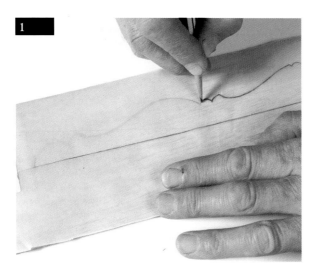

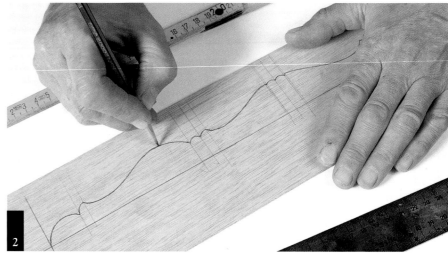

1. The first step is to design the profile of the piece that we wish to turn. Then the profile is drawn on tracing paper or vellum. The paper is then attached to the board with adhesive tape, and the drawing is traced with a pencil to transfer it to the board.

2. When the silhouette of the piece has been marked on the board, it is traced with a pencil so it will be very clear.

3. A symmetrical drawing is achieved by turning the drawing over and repeating the previous steps on the other half of the board.

4. Notice that once the tracing paper has been removed the profile of the piece is light but visible.

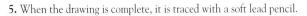

5. When the drawing is complete, it is traced with a soft lead pencil.

6. Finally, using a square, the lines connecting the molding profiles are drawn, completing the drawing of the piece we will make.

7. The wood is then prepared for turning. The pieces are glued together with a sheet of newsprint between them.

8. One of the secrets that ensures a good turning is to glue the parts well; therefore, clamps are used.

9. Once the piece is ready, it is mounted in the lathe to begin the turning process.

10. Notice the difference in size between the two fluted gouges that will be used.

11. We begin to rough out the piece using the larger gouge.

12. The grooves are marked by cutting into the wood with the square chisel.

13. We begin cutting the profile with the square chisel.

14. Notice how the piece begins to take form, following the drawing of the design.

15. The shaping is done using the smaller gouge.

16. It is very important to use a tool rest that is as long as the entire piece.

17. The wood must be sanded after it has been turned. This is done by pressing the sandpaper to the entire piece with the lathe on.

18. We begin waxing the piece without stopping the lathe.

19. The wood is buffed with a cloth so that the finish will be perfect.

20. The two pieces are separated using a square chisel.

21. As the tool enters the wood, it separates without resistance.

22. These half pieces are usually used as decorative appliqués on furniture.

23. The half-round wood pieces are ready to be attached to a piece of furniture.

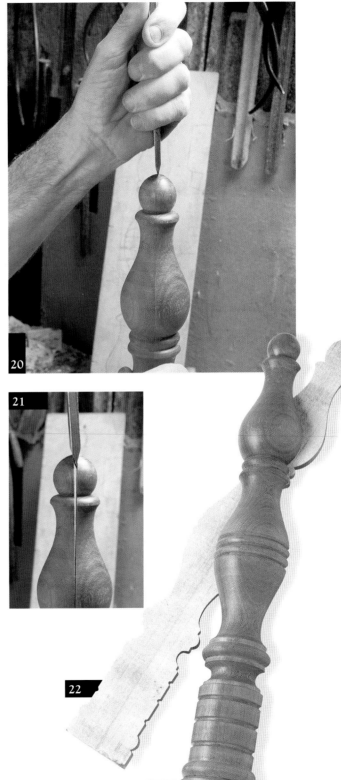

FINISHING ON THE LATHE

One of the most important tasks after turning a piece of wood is deciding the kind of finish that should be applied to it.

Besides the finishes that can be put on the piece after removing it, you should be aware of the possible finishes that can be applied while the piece is still on the lathe. Do not forget that the turner plays an important role in guaranteeing the smoothness of the piece. This section explains sanding, burnishing, burning, and waxing.

Sanding

One of the first finishing tasks of the turner is sanding. This is done by folding the sandpaper and, while the lathe is turning, applying pressure to the wood with the fingertips until the desired smoothness is achieved. At the same time, the sanding will remove all of the tool marks.

On large surfaces, the palm of the hand is rested on the wood, applying pressure with the sandpaper.

When dealing with small profiles keep in mind that they also must be sanded. If necessary, the paper can be folded and inserted into the grooves using the edge for sanding.

1. The turner sands a piece of fir with a medium grade sandpaper.

2. Resting the palm of the hand and the sandpaper on the wood.

3. Sanding small profiles.

Burnishing

The technique of burnishing allows the creation of very smooth surfaces.

Generally, fine steel wool is used for burnishing. The dust that is generated by this finish is very fine. Burnishing can also be done by smoothing the wood with the back of a piece of sandpaper; this technique has been used for quite some time. In the past, a burnished finish was achieved by rubbing the turning piece with wood shavings from the turning process. This technique has been abandoned since the introduction of sanding sponges and steel wool.

4. Burnishing with steel wool.

5. Burnishing can also be done with the back of a sheet of sandpaper.

6. Burnishing with wood shavings.

Burning

Burning the wood is done by making small lines with the parting tool. Then the corner of a piece of wood that is harder than the one on the lathe is pressed firmly into the lines. This type of finish can be used on all pieces of furniture that are made in a rustic style.

Waxing

Waxing is a finish that gives the wood a pleasant feel and great beauty. A piece of wax or paraffin is pressed directly against the piece. It is important to completely cover the entire piece; otherwise, there will be obvious differences in the finish. After impregnating the wood with wax, it should be thoroughly buffed with a cloth; it will begin to shine and look extraordinarily smooth.

7. Burning the wood with friction.

8. This finish is very handsome but somewhat rustic.

9. The wax is applied directly.

10. Thoroughly buffing the wood with a cloth.

MIRROR FRAME

Many wood turning projects require special parts that have to be made by a cabinetmaker. A good turner will explain how the pieces should be made, in order to guarantee that there will not be surprises of any kind during the wood turning process.

The following step-by-step process shows how to make a bull's eye mirror frame, including the preparation of the pieces by the cabinetmaker. The frame made by turning can only be done using this technique, unless a vertical router is used.

MATERIALS and DIMENSIONS

section of the frame

1¼ in (3.2 cm)   2 in (5.2 cm)

detail of the joint

- 4 pieces of walnut 13½ in × 4½ in x 1¼ in (34 × 11 × 3.2 cm)
- plywood board ¼ in (4 mm) thick × 13½ in (33.2 cm) in diameter
- mirror 13 in (33 cm) diameter

1. Once the pieces having the required dimensions for the diameter of the frame have been squared, they are cut with a miter to make the required joints.

2. These joints are strengthened using biscuits that are inserted in grooves made for that purpose.

3. The interior diameter that was previously marked is cut out with a band saw. It is important to remember that the turner will remove part of the wood when making the molding; therefore, the dimensions should be generous.

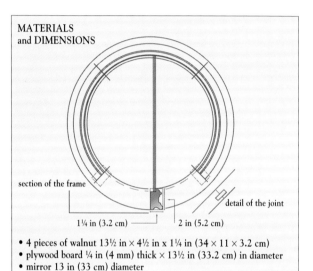

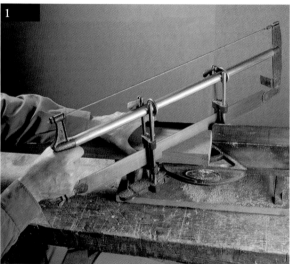

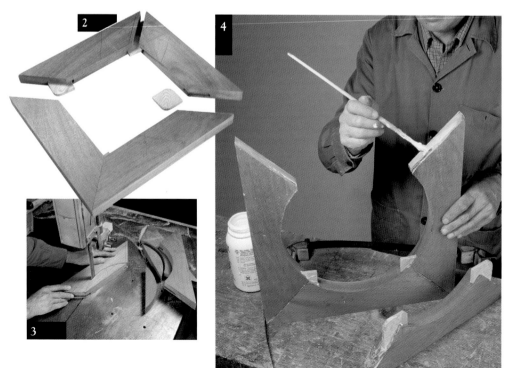

4. The next step consists of gluing together the different pieces with carpenter's glue. At the same time, the biscuits are inserted; it does not matter if they are visible in the inside because the mirror will hide them.

5. Once the glue has set, the outside diameter can be cut with a band saw.

6. To begin turning, find a board, which can be fiberboard, with a diameter close to that of the frame. Measure it with a compass to check the size.

7. This board is attached to the frame on the good side with wood screws.

8. Notice in the detail of the drawing how deep the screws go into the good side of the frame.

9. A faceplate is centered on the fiberboard and attached with lag bolts, which will allow the piece to be mounted to the drive spindle.

10. Material is removed from the outside diameter of the frame using a spindle gouge or a parting tool. In this case, there is very little to remove since the piece is circular. It is very important to watch the position of the gouge, how it is held, and where it is braced during all turning steps.

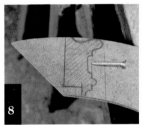

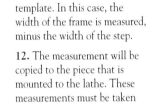

11. The compass can be used to take measurements from a template. In this case, the width of the frame is measured, minus the width of the step.

12. The measurement will be copied to the piece that is mounted to the lathe. These measurements must be taken from the template and are important for making the final piece match the model.

13. Finally, we have only to cut the step using a parting tool. Notice the position of the tool and the hand that supports it.

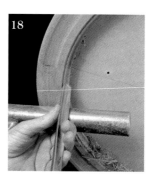

14. To turn the face of the mirror, the frame must be turned over and the other side attached to the fiberboard, using the same screws.

15. When the piece is reattached, it should be centered by tapping it with a hammer so that its rotation will be perfect and the molding flawless.

16. We start by turning the molding in the center part of the edge of the frame. We use the spear-shaped chisel supported on the tool rest.

17. Then the main face of the frame is turned and molded using a gouge. Notice how the position of the tool rest has been changed.

18. With the same tool, the concave molding is shaped on the inside edge of the frame.

19. Finally, only the groove on the face of the frame is left to shape.

20. Different parts of the frame are sanded by applying pressure to the sandpaper with the fingers. In this case, the outside edge is being sanded.

21. The central groove on the face of the frame is sanded in the same manner. As you can see, it would be very difficult to cut this kind of molding on the frame using a router.

22. The rest of the molding is sanded using the same technique.

23. Once the turning of the mirror frame is finished, we cut a board of the same diameter to be used as a back for the frame.

24. The final finish of the frame is a walnut stain applied with a brush.

25. To protect the frame it is necessary to varnish it once the stain has dried. The varnish can be applied with a pad or, as in this case, with a brush.

26. The final look and feel of the frame can be improved by polishing it with fine steel wool or a sanding sponge. Notice that a very fine white powder should be produced during the polishing.

27. When placing the mirror in the frame be careful not to bump it on anything. It should be supported on the lip of the frame that was designed for that purpose.

28. A board cut in the same shape is placed over the mirror and attached with brads. The hammer is slid over the board to avoid damaging the mirror.

29. The finished mirror frame.

CIGAR CONTAINER

*T*urners are true masters because of the specialized techniques that are required in the daily challenges in the shop.

The following project is a good example of this; in it are included the techniques of turning and hollowing a wood piece quite deeply on the inside.

MATERIALS and DIMENSIONS

3 in (7.5 cm)

⅝ in (1.53 cm)
⅝ in (1.51 cm)
⅝ in (1.51 cm)

← 3⅜ in (8.51 cm) →

½ in (1.3 cm)
⅛ in (0.4 cm)

Hollowed 6⅜ in (16 cm) deep by 3⅜ in (8.51 cm) diameter.

7¼ in (18.5 cm)

5⁷⁄₁₆ in (13.8 cm)

³⁄₁₆ in (0.5 cm)
¾ in (2 cm)
³⁄₁₆ in (0.5 cm)

5½ in (14 cm)

• three pieces of cedar 14 in × 6 in × 2 in (35 × 15 × 5 cm)

1. The project begins with the two pieces of faceted cedar wood ready to be turned. The longer piece will be used for the body of the cigar container and the other piece will be the lid.

2. The centers of the two pieces that make up the cigar container are marked with a compass.

3. First, the piece that will become the box is attached to the lathe using the tailstock center.

4. Roughing out begins with a medium gouge while the wood is turning, which will give the piece a cylindrical form. Notice how the turner holds and braces the tool on the tool rest.

5. The wood is removed with a skew chisel to create a spigot that will allow the piece to be held at the end. When planning the project, the piece must be made longer to create the support.

6. The piece is mounted to the lathe again by inserting the spigot into the chuck. This allows us to begin the inside turning.

7. and **8.** The position of the tool rest must be changed to be able to turn the face of the piece.

9. We begin hollowing the wood using the roughing gouge. The tool is moved forward until the center of the piece is reached.

10. Notice that the tool is always angled in the same direction, without changing sides, so it will cut smoothly.

11. Once the hollowing has begun, the inside of the container is deepened and widened using the parting tool. Notice how the turner, besides changing the tool, also holds his hands and braces his tools differently.

12. Here you can see how the different tools make different surfaces. The shape of the inside of the lid was made with a gouge while the shallower outside cut was made with a square chisel.

13. Inside calipers are used to take the dimensions of the interior of the container, which is indicated with dashes.

14. The dimensions should be checked on the piece to compare them to those of the opening on the design drawing.

15. The opening is widened with the parting tool at the same time that it is deepened.

16. If the piece is too thick and the roughing gouge does not reach the bottom, a hole can be drilled in the center of the piece so that the turning can be done with a chisel.

17. Once the hollowing has been done, the inside of the container is thoroughly sanded to finish it. To do this the sandpaper can be rolled around a piece of wood dowel of the required length.

18. The top of the container is turned using the parting tool. The edge of the container should be rounded as this is being done.

19. Use the same tool to shape the profile of the lip at the top of the container following the drawing.

20. Then continue roughing out the outside of the container with the gouge.

21. By folding the drawing in half we can make reference marks for the different molding shapes.

22. Next, we cut in the details that give shape to the piece using the gouge. In this case, we continue roughing out the middle of the outside of the container.

23. As can be seen here, extra wood was left at the bottom of the piece so we can make the molding at the base.

24. We continue using the same gouge to shape this profile.

25. The parting tool leaves a smooth surface but with scrape marks. This is due to the fact that the tool does not cut the wood with its edge.

26. However, we can achieve a smoother surface using the gouge.

27. The piece is thoroughly sanded for a finer finish, taking care to reach all of the corners. Apply pressure with the fingers to achieve a uniform finish.

28. After finishing the sanding, turn the piece around. A special piece of wood has been attached to the live center to be able to do so.

29. The extra wood at the base of the container is removed using the medium gouge.

30. The chisel is used to completely detach the piece from the lathe. This tool leaves the surface of the base perfectly flat.

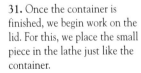

31. Once the container is finished, we begin work on the lid. For this, we place the small piece in the lathe just like the container.

32. The piece is roughed out with the gouge until it is cylindrical in shape.

33. Dimensions are taken from the drawing and checked on the wood piece using the outside calipers. Notice the extra wood for making the molding.

34. Next, the part that is inserted into the container is cut, making sure that the fit will not be too loose.

35. Check the fit between the lid and the container. This step must be done before placing the piece back in the lathe.

36. The dimensions of the molding are transferred to the piece from the drawing as before. A pencil is used for marking.

37. The gouge is used to continue shaping the various moldings on the top of the lid.

38. The finish of the lid is improved with the sanding. Take care to reach all inside corners when doing this.

39 and **40.** This is the way the two pieces look without any type of finishing after they have been sanded. Compare them with the two blocks of wood at the beginning; they turned out beautifully. If wax or another type of finish like varnish is applied afterwards, they will look even better.

SMALL TABLE

Wood turning projects frequently require the duplication of several parts. This is the case in the next project, where we show you how to make a table with three legs, a round top, and bottom shelves.

The featured piece presents the challenge of turning the top, whose diameter is quite large. Norway spruce will be used for this project.

20 in dia. (50 cm)

1⁵⁄₁₆ in (3.3 cm)

21½ in (53.7 cm)

16 in (40 cm)

1⁵⁄₁₆ in (3 cm)

3 in (15 cm)

MATERIALS and DIMENSIONS

- Norway spruce
- table top: 2 pieces 21½ in × 12½ in × 1⁵⁄₁₆ in (55 × 32 × 3.3 cm)
- bottom shelf: 2 pieces 17⅝ in × 9 in × 1⁵⁄₁₆ in (45 × 22 × 3.3 cm)
- legs: 3 pieces 31¼ in × 2 in × 2 in (78 × 5 × 5 cm)

1. A cabinetmaker has prepared the wood pieces that will be used to make the table.

2. The first step consists of preparing the pieces for the lathe. In this case, the centers of the ends of the legs are located using a marking gauge.

3. The awl is tapped with a hammer to make a mark that will help to locate the leg on the lathe.

4. The wood piece is tapped at one end with the hammer to attach it to the lathe. That way the part is held tightly in place.

5. Turning begins right away using a roughing gouge to remove material from the whole piece of wood until a cylindrical shape is created. This tool is used in spindle turning when a large amount of wood has to be removed to achieve a smooth finish. Note that this operation is carried out in most of these projects.

6. Using the cabinetmaker's pattern and a pencil, mark the various measurements of the profile that is to be cut into the legs.

7. The indicated places corresponding to the profile are marked with a straight edged parting tool. Notice that the corner of the sharp edge is used; this allows us to make a small mark in the wood.

8. The spindle gouge is used to make the curved profiles. It is good practice to keep the template with the silhouette being cut within view.

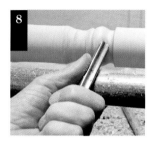

9. The dimensions of one of the legs that has been made are measured with calipers. These dimensions are transferred to the piece being turned. The first piece is made using the dimensions taken from the template.

10. The lower part of the table leg is shaped with the chisel. Remember the importance of the position of the hands, the bracing of the tool, and the movement of the handle during all wood turning tasks.

11. The same tool is used to mark and shape several profiles. In this case the bead that is at the upper part of the leg is being turned.

12. The middle part of the leg is then turned using the spindle gouge.

13. Notice the similarity between the shape of the model and the leg achieved by using a fairly large gouge.

14. Finally, the wood should be rubbed with sandpaper to eliminate all of the possible imperfections caused by the gouges.

15. Just like in the straight areas, the various moldings are sanded while applying pressure with the finger tips.

16. The tenon is formed by cutting away the wood using a spear point chisel. This will be used to join the legs to the tabletop.

17. Using a gauge, the diameter of the tenon is checked to adjust it to the model.

18. When the piece has been sanded in one direction, a fuzz is raised that affects the smoothness. Therefore, the wood part is reversed to change the direction of the sanding.

19. We continue sanding the entire surface of the leg just as previously described to make it smooth.

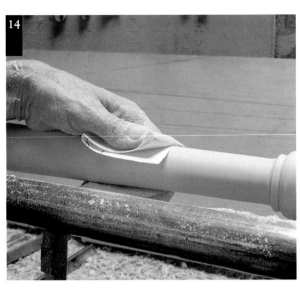

20. All that remains is to cut off the end with the straight edged parting tool. Follow these steps to make the rest of the legs.

21. Before beginning to turn the circular pieces of the table, mark the center and the positions of the legs using dividers.

22. The faceplate is placed over the piece; holes are made with a hammer and an awl to help start the screws that attach the faceplate to the wood.

23. Before turning the table top, and as we have just described, the wood is attached to the faceplate with lag bolts.

24. We begin removing wood with a straight chisel; this operation should be done carefully because we are working with the end grain.

25. On occasion, instead of watching the tool that is being used, the turner watches the top of the piece, where it is easier to see the shape of the molding.

26. Notice how the molding begins to appear. The last step will be sanding.

27. As you can see, because of the diameter of the piece, it has to be turned on a lathe located at the far end of the bench.

28. The wood is turned with a gouge to shape the molding in the top edge of the tabletop.

29. Observe in this close-up how the tool is rested and the position of the turner's hands against the tool rest.

30. Use the dividers to take measurements from the template, which is drawn at full scale.

31. These dimensions are transferred to the piece that is being turned. Notice that the dividers are held against the tool rest.

32. The spear point chisel can also be used to remove material to begin cutting some of the molding.

33. Then final touches are made with the spindle gouge.

34. The piece is thoroughly sanded to achieve a better finish, making sure to reach all the corners of the molding. The bottom shelf of the table is turned following the same steps as those for the tabletop.

35. When all of the pieces have been turned, the turner passes his work to the cabinet-maker so he or she can do the final assembly.

36. First, the required joints are marked using a template, then the joints are cut out and holes made for the dowels in the bottom shelf of the table.

37. When the holes have been drilled, glue is applied to the dowels and all the parts are assembled.

38. After gluing, the table is adjusted and clamped. A filler can be applied while the glue is drying.

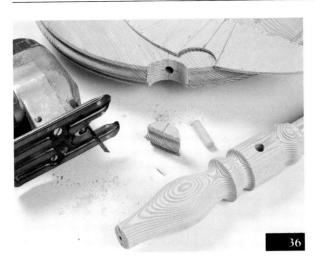

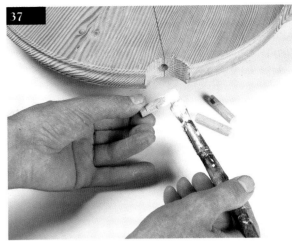

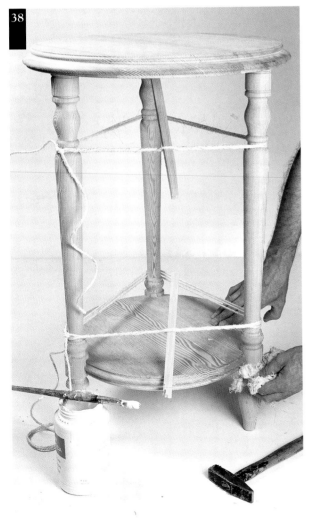

39. Notice the difference in color and contrast in the wood grain caused by the varnish.

40. Next the flat surfaces are polished with an electric sander and the curves and molding are sanded by hand.

41. The surface is waxed to finalize the process of finishing the table.

42. Finally, we can appreciate the results of the work done by two great professionals, the turner and the cabinetmaker.

WOODEN BALL

*I*n this case we will develop a decorative element consisting of a ball made of a light fir and a darker walnut. This sphere will rest on a pedestal made of walnut. As is the case in most wood turning projects, it is first necessary to have a cabinetmaker prepare the different pieces of wood according to the instructions of the turner.

MATERIALS and DIMENSIONS

BALL
- 2 fir boards 9 in × 8 in × 2⅞ in (22 × 20 × 7 cm)
- 2 walnut boards 9 in × 8 in × 2⅞ in (22 × 20 × 7 cm)
- diameter: 7⅞ in (19.5 cm)

2⅝" (6.5 cm)

4⅞" (12 cm)

PEDESTAL
- 1 piece of walnut wood 5 in × 5 in × 3 in (13 × 13 × 7.5 cm)

1. The project begins with a preparatory task consisting of cutting the different kinds of wood diagonally on edge. A band saw is used for this.

2. Then the pieces are stacked alternating the colors and gluing them with carpenter's glue. To temporarily hold them drive some finishing nails through the narrow parts of all of them so they do not move when pressure is applied.

3. Pressure is applied to the whole stack using clamps. This gluing operation is very important, because if it is not done well the wood will splinter when being turned.

4. Once the glue has set, cut off the corners of the stack of glued pieces at the point where they were nailed together with the finishing nails.

5. The shaping of the piece will make it easier for the turner to begin to work on the object that he or she has to make.

6. A piece of walnut wood is prepared for the pedestal, also with the corners cut off.

7. The first task of the turner is to place the part on the lathe after marking its centers. Notice that spigots have been glued to the ends of the piece to allow its full use.

8. The turning of the ball is done with a chisel. In this case, we do not recommend using a gouge, because the direction of the wood grain would cause splintering.

9. Notice that stock is removed starting from the middle and moving to the ends.

10. Hold the tool firmly while turning and forming the shape of the sphere.

11. Once the sides of the sphere have been formed, the position of the tool rest should be changed before beginning to turn the ends.

12. We continue turning with the chisel following the same steps as before.

13. Observe how the spigots are cut down to facilitate the shaping of the end of the piece.

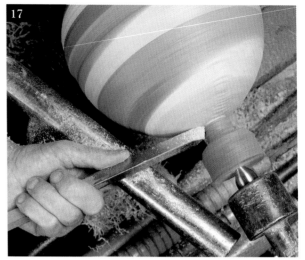

14. Once the piece has been roughed out, we continue shaping it with a roughing gouge. Notice that the finish is much smoother.

15. A line is drawn on the center of the ball for reference.

16. The shaping of the ball is finished with the gouge.

17. Alternate the shaping of the ball and the removal of material from the spigots.

18. The diameters of the ball are checked using outside calipers.

19. The same checking continues in various directions.

20. Next, the piece can be sanded using a medium grit sandpaper. Notice how both hands are used to apply pressure while sanding.

21. From time to time, the piece is turned around to sand it in the other direction, thus avoiding raising the grain of the wood.

22. The sanding is done the same way as before.

23. Finally, all that is left is to finish the piece by applying pure beeswax. This task is carried out while the piece is turning.

24. Then pressure is applied to the ball with a cloth. The heat will melt the wax and spread it over the surface.

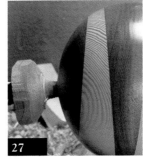

25. As you can see, this type of glossy finish really stands out.

26. The spigot is cut down a little bit more in order to remove the ball and finish it.

27. When the connections of the spigots are narrow enough, stop cutting and turn off the lathe.

28. Now the piece can be removed from the lathe.

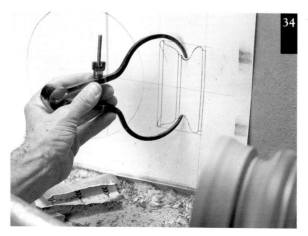

29. The excess wood is removed with a chisel.

30. The finish on the ends is touched up with sandpaper.

31. To start the second part of the project, take the piece that will become the base and find its center with a set of dividers.

32. The roughing out and rounding of the base is done with a straight-edged chisel.

33. The gouge is used to shape the edge of the pedestal.

34. Use the outside calipers to measure the dimensions on the reference drawing.

35. The dimensions taken from the drawing are checked against the piece that is being turned.

36. The molding profile on the base is finished with the gouge.

37. Next, using the same gouge, the inside of the base is hollowed. Do this by working from outside to inside. Notice the position of the turner's hands during this operation.

38. The surface is sanded to prepare the piece for the final finish.

39. The base is waxed and vigorously buffed with a rag in the same way as the ball.

40. The completed ball.

41. The finished pedestal is ready to hold the ball.

42. The completed decorative piece consisting of the ball and the pedestal.

GARDEN URN

*T*o make this bell-shaped garden urn requires a high level of precision in the turning of all of the pieces so that they fit into each other perfectly. The preliminary work of the cabinetmaker is also complicated, because each one of the shapes must conform to the urn in its rough shape. Throughout the entire project, it is very important to carefully watch the position of the hands and of the tools, as well as the bracing of these on the tool rest. The success of the final object will often depend on these small details.

MATERIALS and DIMENSIONS

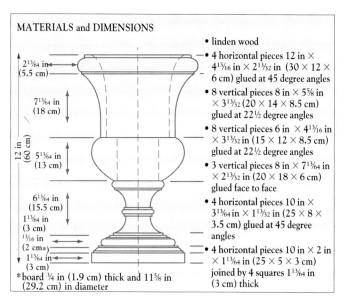

- linden wood
- 4 horizontal pieces 12 in × 4^{13}/$_{16}$ in × 2^{13}/$_{32}$ in (30 × 12 × 6 cm) glued at 45 degree angles
- 8 vertical pieces 8 in × 5^{5}/$_{8}$ in × 3^{13}/$_{32}$ in (20 × 14 × 8.5 cm) glued at 22½ degree angles
- 8 vertical pieces 6 in × 4^{13}/$_{16}$ in × 3^{13}/$_{32}$ in (15 × 12 × 8.5 cm) glued at 22½ degree angles
- 3 vertical pieces 8 in × 7^{13}/$_{64}$ in × 2^{13}/$_{32}$ in (20 × 18 × 6 cm) glued face to face
- 4 horizontal pieces 10 in × 3^{13}/$_{64}$ in × 1^{13}/$_{32}$ in (25 × 8 × 3.5 cm) glued at 45 degree angles
- 4 horizontal pieces 10 in × 2 in × 1^{13}/$_{64}$ in (25 × 5 × 3 cm) joined by 4 squares 1^{13}/$_{64}$ in (3 cm) thick

Dimensions shown on diagram:
2^{13}/$_{64}$ in (5.5 cm)
7^{13}/$_{64}$ in (18 cm)
12 in (60 cm)
5^{13}/$_{64}$ in (13 cm)
6^{13}/$_{64}$ in (15.5 cm)
1^{13}/$_{64}$ in (3 cm)
^{13}/$_{16}$ in (2 cm*)
1^{13}/$_{64}$ in (3 cm)

*board ¾ in (1.9 cm) thick and 11⅝ in (29.2 cm) in diameter

1. The silhouette of the urn before it has been roughed out is similar to the intended profile of the finished piece. All of the parts can be seen in it. Besides the lathe, gouges and sandpaper are needed for modeling the urn.

2. The first part to be turned is the ring that sits on top of the urn.

3. The part is first placed on the lathe's faceplate, making sure to line up both centers.

4. Screws are used to attach the piece that we are going to turn to the faceplate.

5. The piece is adjusted on the faceplate by lightly tapping with a hammer to ensure that it rotates properly.

6. Then the lathe is started and the roughing out and profiling of the edge is done with a chisel.

7. A gouge is used to turn the inside of the top ring. Notice the position of the gouge and the turner's hands in carrying out this task.

8. The gouge is also used to rough out the outermost side of the face of the ring.

9. To finish shaping the face of the ring closer to the center, hold the tool firmly in order to apply more pressure.

10. Finally, the face of the ring is sanded by passing the sandpaper across the profile of the piece.

11. The edge of the ring is sanded in the same manner. Keep in mind that it is important to work with the fingertips to preserve the shapes.

12. Once the ring is finished, we take the body of the cone that will be attached underneath the ring.

13. The inside diameter of the ring is marked on the wide end of the cone with a pencil.

14. The piece is centered and adjusted on the lathe with a few taps of the hammer.

15. The inside of the bell is roughed out with a chisel so that it will fit into the ring.

16. Next, the piece is turned around. We are then ready to begin turning the outside of the bell.

17. The body of the bell is roughed out with the chisel.

18. A lip is formed at the bottom of the bell so it can be inserted into the center piece. Notice how the tool is braced.

19. The final silhouette of the piece is turned using the roughing gouge.

20. A smooth surface is achieved by rolling the gouge to the left and right.

21. With the lathe still in motion, we begin to polish it with sandpaper until the desired smoothness is achieved.

22. The center piece of the urn is connected to the base of the bell.

23. The roughing gouge can be used when we begin to shape a piece without sharp corners.

24. To determine the fit between the pieces a caliper is used to measure the inside diameter of the lip.

25. When transferring the dimensions to the new piece with calipers, carefully mark the bar with the point that is braced on the tool rest.

26. The diameter of the insert is cut with the chisel.

27. Smooth and check to see that the two pieces fit together perfectly.

28. The base of the urn is turned next.

29. The center of the piece is found using the dividers, which are tapped with a hammer to mark it.

30. The piece is shaped using the spindle turning technique.

31. We begin rounding the corners using the chisel.

32. The profile of the molded edge is completed using the roughing gouge.

33. The chisel is used when turning the end grain of the piece.

34. The middle part of the piece is roughed out using the roughing gouge. As you can see, the bead around the middle is becoming visible.

35. The diameter of the piece should be frequently checked using the outside calipers.

36. You can see that the turning of the lower curved area begins at one side.

37. Hold the tool tightly as you get closer to the middle part of the radius.

38. The removal of material and shaping with the gouge is finished when you get to the bead in the middle.

39. The corners of the central bead are shaped with a chisel.

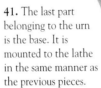

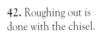

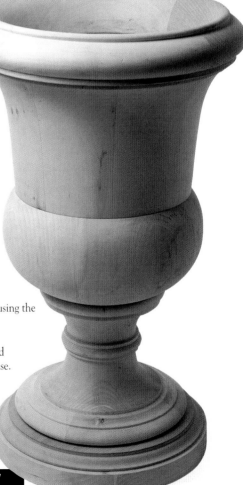

40. The finished and polished piece can be seen still on the lathe.

41. The last part belonging to the urn is the base. It is mounted to the lathe in the same manner as the previous pieces.

42. Roughing out is done with the chisel.

43. The shaping of the molding is done with the same tool.

44. The profile of the molding is completed using the gouge.

45. The completed and polished garden urn base.

46. Gluing up the various parts of the urn.

47. The completed garden urn.

STOOL

*T*his three-legged oak stool has been left for last because it entails a series of turning operations that require special skills and abilities, like threading and tapping. As you have seen in the previous projects, a great degree of cooperation is needed between the turner and the cabinetmaker in order for the project to turn out successfully.

13 in seat diameter (32.5 cm)

2⅛ in (5.3 cm)

20⅞ in (53 cm)

MATERIALS and DIMENSIONS

- solid oak
- seat: 2 pieces 15 in × 6¾ in × 2⅜ in (35 × 17 × 6 cm)
- legs: 3 pieces 20⅞ in × 2¾ in × 2¾ in (53 × 6 × 6 cm)
- threaded pieces: 3 pieces 4 in × 3³⁄₁₆ in × 1⅝ in (10 × 8 × 4 cm)
- threaded dowels: ½ in diameter and 8 in long (1.2 × 20 cm)

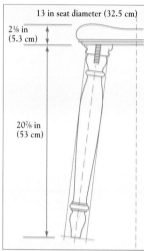

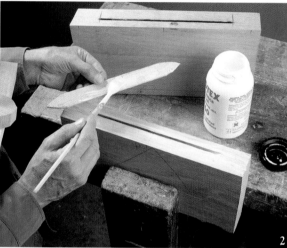

1. As always, and as in any wood turning project, the parts that are to be turned have to be prepared by a carpenter or cabinetmaker. In this case, three legs, three connecting pieces, and the seat of the stool are required.

2. Due to its size, the seat of the stool cannot be made of a single piece of wood; it will be necessary to join two pieces using a special biscuit. Notice that this is not centered in the thickness, so that material can be removed from the side that has more wood.

3. After applying glue to the two pieces, they are held with two clamps to help the glue bond perfectly.

4. In order to make the turning of large pieces easier, the carpenter cuts the piece into a circle, leaving enough wood for the turner to rough out the perimeter and shape the edge.

5. Finally, with all of the parts prepared and either a full-scale drawing or patterns based on the drawing of the stool made, the wood turning work can begin.

6. The project begins with the seat of the stool. As always, the piece must be prepared for the lathe; first the center of the piece is marked so the faceplate can be attached.

7. Holes are made in the piece with a hand drill or an awl to attach it to the plate.

8. It is attached with screws and washers and tightened using a wrench.

9. Once the plate is attached to the lathe, the turner spins the piece to see that it rotates perfectly; if not, it is balanced with light taps of a hammer.

10. The seat is turned on the faceplate using a spear point chisel or parting tool, because the end grain is being worked.

11. The shaping of the top of the seat is done using a roughing gouge, removing more material from the middle area. To do so the turning is done beginning in the center.

12. Bracing the chisel on the tool rest, the decorative molded profile is cut on the edge of the seat. Notice that the drawing with the dimensions of the stool is always near the turner, so that he or she can check it and compare it to the piece.

13. Then the gouge is moved toward the outside edge.

14. To check the depth of the cut, a ruler and a perfectly straight stick are used.

15. The edge of the seat is rounded using the roughing gouge.

16. The final touching up of the rounded shape is done with the parting tool or a scraper. The experience and skill of the turner are essential to this type of task.

17. A general view of the position of the turner when he or she is working the wood to smooth the concave center of the seat.

18. The last step consists of polishing the piece until the desired smoothness is achieved. To do so, while the lathe is turning, sandpaper is firmly held against the moving piece.

19. The next step is the turning of the legs of the stool. Before turning them, the centers are marked with a marking gauge.

20. The following tasks are necessary to make the hole in the leg for a threaded dowel that corresponds to another piece with female threads, which is attached to the seat of the stool.

A drill bit is placed in the chuck of the lathe to drill a hole in the leg so it can be threaded. Notice the shop drawing.

21. For drilling the hole, the bit is inserted into the leg by turning the hand wheel of the tailstock.

22. The piece with the female thread is made of oak. As always, the process begins by marking the centers of the pieces.

23. The piece is drilled using a bit approximately the same diameter as that of the female threads.

24. The next step consists of making the male threads. For this, material is removed from two blocks of wood until they are cylindrical.

25. The gauge is used to accurately mark the desired diameter of the dowel.

26. It is a good idea to coat the pieces to be threaded with petroleum jelly, and let it penetrate for 24 hours. This will allow the wood to turn easily in the thread chaser.

27. During those 24 hours, the turner works to prepare for the turning of the legs. The dimensions are taken directly from the shop drawing and are marked on a board.

28. It is also a good idea to prepare different calipers, set to different diameters, to speed up the work.

29. Once the oak has been placed in the lathe, it can be roughed out with the gouge until a perfectly cylindrical piece is achieved.

30. To shape the different parts of the leg, the dimensions are taken from the previously marked board and marked on the leg while the lathe is turning.

31. Begin by marking the different shapes of the molding with the chisel.

32. Then using the large caliper, the diameters of the piece are checked to ensure they are the same on all of the legs.

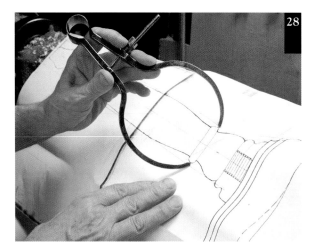

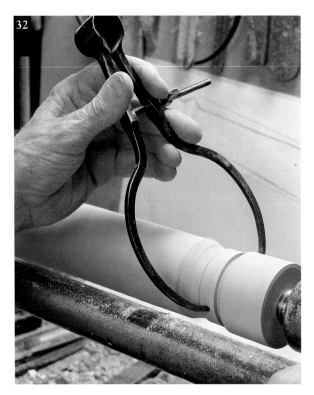

33. For a better finish, the pieces are given a pass with the chisel. The wood disappears as the tool moves along the leg.

34. The leg is always turned with the chisel from the outermost point towards the bead, so the bead is well defined.

35. The lower part of the leg is shaped with the roughing gouge. Dimensions and diameters are checked in the same way as on the upper end of the leg.

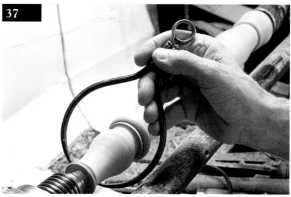

36. The chisel is used to impart a smoother finish.

37. Finally, the diameters of the different parts of the leg are checked.

38. Next, another leg is turned, following the same steps as on the first. The process must be repeated three times.

39. Because we are working with oak, it must be sanded in both directions to eliminate the raised grain.

40. Then the male threads are made with the thread chaser. First, the piece of wood is introduced into the tool while off the lathe.

41. Then the piece is attached to the lathe and the threading is continued carefully.

42. Notice how the threads turn out.

43. Keep in mind that the belt that turns the pulleys must be held with one hand so that the live center will not move.

44. When the thread has been finished, material is removed with a parting tool to create cylindrical dowels.

45. Three threaded dowels are made from the previously prepared cylinder.

46. With the reference drawing it is easy to see that the threaded dowel goes into the top end of the leg.

47. To make the female threads in the pieces that are to be attached to the bottom of the seat, clamp them to the workbench and use the tap.

48. An auxiliary piece with threads is made to allow the seat joints to be attached to the lathe and turned.

49. The auxiliary piece is screwed into the seat joint and both are then attached to the lathe.

50. The lower part of the piece is shaped with a spear point chisel.

51. The roughing gouge is used to shape the central part of the piece.

52. Next, we sand the contact point of the intermediate piece that goes between the legs and the seat. The sanding is done on a plate with sandpaper that is attached to the lathe. Notice the angle of the piece.

53. It is always a good idea to check dimensions with different measuring instruments. In this case, calipers are used.

54. Carpenter's glue is used to attach the dowel to the leg. The piece is inserted part way into the seat joint to apply the glue.

55. A view of the assembly of the leg, seat joint, and threaded dowel.

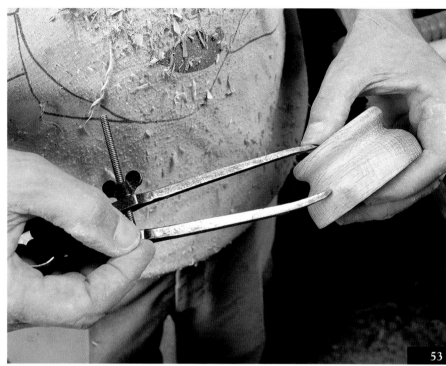

56. The seat joint is glued to the seat of the stool and reinforced with screws.

57. A view of the finished stool.

GLOSSARY

Appliqué. A piece that is used to complement a decoration.

Awl. Steel instrument with a sharp point. Used for making holes and marking pieces.

Bed. The large bench that the lathe rests on.

Blunt. An obtuse form without a point.

Burnish. To shine or polish metal, stone, wood, etc.

Clamp. A tool used for holding or applying force to a piece on a workbench or to two pieces of wood.

Curing. The process of solidification of the liquid element of a conglomerate.

Drive center. Produces the movement of the lathe.

Edge. Angled cut on the blade of any cutting tool.

End grain. The surface resulting from sawing a piece of wood perpendicular to the direction of the wood grain.

Flute. Concave shape, whose profile is generally a semicircle.

Fracture. To break or split.

Fuzz. A flaw in wood caused by a change in the direction of the fibers, causing them to be raised when the piece is worked.

Gouge. A basic tool used in wood turning. Generally denotes a chisel with a sharpened, curved blade.

Hilo. A cut made in wood following the direction of the grain of the wood.

Joinery. The assembling of wood parts.

Molding. Ornament with a specific profile that is used in cabinetmaking projects.

Nogalina. A stain that is made from walnut shells and is used by dissolving in water to imitate the color of walnut wood.

Polish. To remove the grain that has been raised on a piece of wood to make the remaining wood smoother.

Rough out. To remove large parts of any material that is being worked. In wood turning, roughing out is the first operation.

Sanding. Rubbing wood with an abrasive paper to make it smooth.

Scale. A measured, proportional representation. Size or proportion used for developing a design.

Shaping. To give form or to cut a profile in a material.

Spigot. Extra material on the end of an object that allows it to be attached to something.

Splinter. A fragment thrown from a piece of wood or wood object that breaks or comes apart in a violent manner.

Step. The groove that the edge of a part or decorative piece fits into.

Staining. To color a piece of wood without covering or obscuring the wood grain.

Template. Board or pattern on which is marked the shape and the sizes required for the surface of a piece, and, when placed on it, is used in different ways as a ruler for cutting or working it.

Turning. Working or rounding a piece of material on a lathe.

Varnish. Liquid mixture that is applied in thin coats and forms a solid transparent film.

Waxing. Covering furniture or wood objects with a thin coat of wax.

White glue (also known as Carpenter's glue). Adhesive paste that is used in cabinetmaking, carpentry, and generally in all trades that use wood.

Wood boring insect. A term for insects that eat away wood.

Wood grain. The stratification of the wood fibers in a piece of wood.

Wood shavings. A fine, curled wood chip produced by working wood with cutting tools.